Old GIRVAN

by

Hugh Maxwell

A Durham–Churchill charabanc, pictured outside the King's Arms Hotel in Dalrymple Street. The proprietor of the hotel was Thomas Lees who ran 'Coast and Country' tours, initially using horse-drawn stagecoaches and later, with the advent of the motor vehicle, charabancs. In this photograph a man can be seen holding the bugle, a leftover from the horse-drawn days which was used to warn other road users of the stagecoach's approach. An advertisement published in a local journal in 1906 stated: 'King's Arms Hotel, Girvan. The principal family and commercial hotel. Headquarters of the famed Girvan, Ballantrae and Colmonell coaching tour. Coaches running daily from April till September, leaving hotel at 10.30 a.m. – thirty miles through the most magnificent scenery. Motor charabanc running daily during season. For full particulars of the various runs apply at hotel. Thos. Lees, Proprietor.'

ISBN 1 84033 239 5

The publishers regret that they cannot supply
copies of any pictures featured in this book.

FURTHER READING
The books listed below were used by the author during his research.
None of them are available from Stenlake Publishing. Those interested
in finding out more are advised to contact their local bookshop or
reference library.

Rob Close, *Ayrshire & Arran – An Illustrated Architectural Guide*,
    1992.
The Rev. R. Lawson, *Places of Interest about Girvan*, 1892.
The Rev. R. Lawson, *Views of Carrick*, 1894.
James Mackenna, *Round about Girvan*, 1906.
J. Kevan McDowall, *Carrick Gallovidian*, 1947.
Rotary Club of Girvan, *Girvan 1668–2000*, 2000.
James Edward Shaw, *Ayrshire 1745–1950: A Social and Industrial
    History of the County*, 1953.
John Strawhorn, *Ayrshire – the Story of a County*, 1975.

ACKNOWLEDGEMENTS
The author wishes to thank the staffs of the reference departments at
the Dick Institute, Kilmarnock, the Carnegie Library, Ayr, and the staffs
of the Local History Library in Ardrossan and Girvan Library. He
would also like to acknowledge the invaluable help of the many people
living in Girvan, particularly Gordon Clark, who willingly contributed
information towards this book, and also the Girvan Tourist Office.

    The publishers wish to thank the following for contributing
photographs to this book: Gordon Clark for pages 2, 4, 6, 9–20, 22–24,
27, 30, 31, 33–35, 37–39, 43 (both), 44, 45, 47 and 48; Alex McGowan
for the front cover, pages 8, 21, 25, 26, 28, 29, 32, 36, 40, 41 and the
inside back cover; and Malcolm Chadwick for pages 5 and 42.

Gordon's Dairy is situated at 27 Hamilton Street and was established
in 1892 by Adam Gordon who was a self-employed worker at
Dunnymuck Farm near Girvan. In this photograph Adam's son John,
who carried on the business, can be seen on the left standing in the
doorway of the shop. Today the Gordon family still own the same
shop, selling milk, general groceries and even toys. Milk is also still
delivered daily to doors throughout the town and surrounding area
as it has been for over a hundred years.

INTRODUCTION

Girvan was originally named 'Invergarvane' which derives from the Gaelic *Inbhir Gearraidh Abhainn* – 'the mouth of the river gully' – and over successive centuries this name has become corrupted and shortened; in former times the town was called 'Garvan', 'Gyruen' and 'Girvane'.

Ancient life was recorded in the *New Statistical Account* of 1845 when the parish minister noted that 'formerly there were a number of cairns in the high part of the parish, but these have been almost wholly demolished for the purpose of making fences.' Artefacts dating from the Bronze Age were also discovered and numerous hill forts or duns were constructed at Dinvin, Dowhill, Motehill, Trowier, the Doune Knoll and on north Daltippan Hill.

Knockushion, an area which now overlooks the harbour, was also once a Moot Hill or 'a moat' of justice as it was formerly the site of the principal court in the Earldom of Carrick. On 6 February 1328 – a year prior to his death – Robert the Bruce himself reputedly held court there. However, by Act of Parliament the head court of the Bailiary of Carrick was transferred to Maybole in 1639.

From earliest times the estuary of the river was much frequented by fisherman and their families from Ireland and the Highlands. They settled in the area and soon a small clachan developed under the guidance of the church which was erected by Duncan, Earl of Carrick, near the end of the twelfth century. There also seems to have been a bridge at Girvan, spanning the river as early as the close of the sixteenth century. A hostile encounter is said to have once occurred at 'the brig of Girwand' between two of the powerful feudal families of Ayrshire, although by the close of the seventeenth century the bridge seems to have either decayed or been swept away. Emphasising its importance to the town, the Presbytery of Ayr sent a letter to Lord Bargany, dated 4 March 1696, requesting the building of a new bridge across the river near the new church and this was constructed shortly afterwards.

Girvan could have become a burgh of barony in 1668 when a charter was granted to Mr Thomas Boyd of Ballochtoul. Boyd designed streets and marked them out in the barren sands on the south side of the Water of Girvan, even erecting a pole to mark the site of the burgh cross. But his designs were never implemented and not a single house was built. The charter for the burgh of barony was further renewed in 1696 for Sir Archibald Muir of Thornton, but again the community failed to increase beyond the size of an obscure coastal hamlet.

By 1700 Girvan still only had about twenty to thirty houses containing around one hundred people. However, by the mid-1700s herring fishing had become a major industry and this caused a dramatic rise in population to about a thousand. At this time landowners near the coast and throughout Ayrshire were also introducing many revolutionary agricultural reforms and families that were displaced from the old overcrowded fermtouns took up residence in the town. Smuggling also took place along the coast and many of those who actively participated in this lucrative, but illicit, activity settled in Girvan.

The original burgh charter granted to Girvan continued in abeyance until 1785 when, as a result of its growth in size, the then proprietor of the land, Mr Hamilton of Bargany, decided to exercise its privileges. Under his direction Girvan finally became a burgh of barony, governed by two annually elected bailies and a council of ten local gentlemen.

The introduction of handloom weaving also brought further prosperity and according to the *Statistical Account of Scotland* of 1794 a hundred looms were at work in the town. By 1810 it had become one of Ayrshire's principal muslin centres and had 500 weavers. The population again increased dramatically so that by the mid-1800s there were 2,000 handlooms spinning the web. There also began a large influx of Ulster Irish immigrant workers to the district, many of whom settled within the town and found work either in fishing, agriculture or within the cotton trade. By 1850 the population peaked at 8,659.

Throughout the nineteenth century the harbour and the fishing fleet were developed so that the town became the principal seaport of Carrick, with exports being made annually of grain, coal, lime, potatoes and many other commodities. The building of small fishing craft and trading schooners was also an important industry.

In 1860 the railway reached Girvan and from that point the town began its development as a holiday resort. A second railway line, opened in 1906, increased this potential and by 1910 thousands of visitors saw Girvan as a place of resort away from the noisy and polluted industrial centres of central Scotland. During the Glasgow Fair Week, the town's population of around 6,000 would swell to nearer 16,000. However, after 1900 the town's population dropped to 4,872 due to the replacement of handloom weaving by machine production within large purpose-built factories. The port also declined in trade as the fishing industry entered a slump and ships became too large to safely negotiate the pronounced bar at the entrance to the harbour.

Despite these setbacks the council built around six hundred houses during the inter-war period and efforts were made to increase the town's resort potential. The promenade was constructed, along with ornamental ponds for paddling and motor boating, greens for golf, putting, cricket and bowling, beautiful gardens, pavilions, an outdoor gymnasium and even a fairground with amusements.

After the Second World War the council again undertook extensive house building with many schemes being built and numerous dilapidated properties being replaced or renovated. The population began to slowly increase once again, reaching 7,000 by 1948. In 1963 William Grant and Sons, the producers of Glenfiddich malt whisky, began large-scale grain distilling just north of Girvan at Grangestone. Ladyburn malt whisky distillery was added three years later, but closed in 1975. Grangestone is still in operation.

Today, the population has stabilised at around 8,000 and the town still attracts visitors during the summer months, despite many people now choosing to travel abroad on holiday. Beautifully situated with its fine sandy beach, magnificent views across the Firth of Clyde to Ailsa Craig, Arran and the Mull of Kintyre, Girvan still has plenty to offer and remains one of the principal destinations on the west coast for day trippers.

In this photograph of the harbour a large catch of cod has been laid out for sale on the harbour side. Tables for dressing the fish and the wooden barrels that were used to cure and store the salted cod are alongside. In the background are Knockushion Gardens which were created on the site of some old houses – known as 'The Follies' – around 1912. Beyond the gardens the tower known as 'Auld Stumpy' and the McMaster Hall stand at the junction of Dalrymple Street. Just out of view to the left, towering to a height of 150 feet, is the spire of the North Parish Church which, designed by William G. Rowan, was built in Montgomerie Street in 1884 at a cost of £5,000. Just out of picture on the right is Harbour Place and the junction of Henrietta Street where an ironworks once stood. At the harbour side was Carson's, the fish and ice merchant who also specialised in fresh game and poultry, while still at the corner of the junction to Henrietta Street is the Harbour Bar which dates from the early nineteenth century.

This remarkable fish, possibly a rare tuna, was caught outside Girvan Harbour on 10 July 1915. Although little is known locally of the story behind its capture, it is recorded that the fish weighed in at an incredible 644lbs and had a length of seven feet and six inches and a girth of six feet. On Thursday, 18 March 1909 the *Ayr Advertiser* declared that there had been a 'Royal Sturgeon Captured' – 'A small specimen of the royal sturgeon, a rare fish, which can be claimed for the King's table, was landed in Girvan on Saturday. It was caught by Mr Alexander Muir in a cod net, about two miles from Ailsa Craig. It was three feet ten inches in length and fifteen inches in girth. This interesting creature is

a rare visitor to the Firth of Clyde, this being the first specimen landed at Girvan. Some years ago a royal sturgeon was caught at Turnberry.' The harbour was often an area bustling with activity, with many vessels coming and going as they landed their valuable catches. The *Carrick Directory*, published in 1883, detailed why: 'The Girvan herring has become a favourite delicacy in the large cities of England . . . . From December until the end of March, the Bay is covered with boats from all the fishing stations in the kingdom . . . [and] attracted during one season more than 1,400 fishermen and the total value of the fish caught amounted to nearly £100,000. To meet the demands of this growing traffic, the proprietors of the harbour – the Earl of Stair, Mr Kennedy of Dalquharran, and the Glasgow and South Western Railway Company – have been induced to enlarge and improve its accommodation for boats and it is now in the course of being deepened, widened and protected by a breakwater. The works, now approaching completion, will render the harbour a safe and commodious haven for ships of considerable tonnage, and hopes are entertained that a portion of the Irish traffic will seek this convenient port.'

Small boats and fishing craft were originally employed in ferrying holidaymakers from Girvan across to Ailsa Craig, but by 1906 Mr A. Girvan operated the small steamer *Ailsa* on the route. She proved popular with tourists and in 1924 the steamship *Ailsa II* entered service, although she was quickly renamed the *Lady Ailsa*. Built at Ayr by the Ailsa Shipbuilding Company and powered by engines constructed by A. Hall and Co. in Aberdeen, she sailed regularly during the summer months from the harbour at Girvan to Ailsa Craig and even to Arran. This photograph was taken from near the end of the pier and shows the steamship leaving the harbour, crowded with passengers. In the background are the large villas built alongside the golf course on Watermouth Park. At Ailsa Craig a small pier was built to safely land visitors, but during the inter-war years the service proved less profitable and the *Lady Ailsa* was sold in 1932. However, only two years later another vessel, also named *Lady Ailsa*, began to operate on the route. A smaller fishing-style boat replaced the larger vessel in 1955 and was operated by Mr I. Girvan, the grandson of the original founder of the service.

A large crowd watches the spectacular launching of the lifeboat around 1910. On the right are the large wheels of the horse-drawn cart that carried the vessel to the water. On Thursday, 24 July 1913 the *Ayr Advertiser* reported that in Girvan 'Saturday was easily the busiest day of the season so far, thousands of people thronging the principal thoroughfares. The local lifeboat, managed by the crew under the charge of Captain D. Muir, was mounted on a lorry and taken through the town. Accompanying the boat were the Brownies, who, with long poles with bags attached to the end, spared no effort to entice the humble coppers from the crowds to help the funds of the National Lifeboat Institution. After proceeding through the principal thoroughfares, headed by the Girvan Pipe Band, the lifeboat was taken to the harbour, where, in the presence of hundreds of visitors, it was launched, and after a short sail on the Firth returned to the harbour.'

LAUNCHING the LIFEBOAT.

RIDDEL, PHOTO. GIRVAN.

A lifeboat has been stationed at Girvan since 13 January 1865 when a small lifeboat house was constructed near the harbour by the Duchesse de Coigny. Initially, when it was a boat with sails and oars, it was launched from the sandy beach in front of what is now Louisa Drive and was either pulled there by horses or more usually by teams of boys. When people were resident on Ailsa Craig the lifeboat responded to emergencies and messages were either received by pigeon flying to the dovecot located at the harbour or by coloured distress flares lit on Ailsa Craig itself. The first lifeboat was named *The Earl of Carrick*; this was later renamed the *Sir Home Popham* and it remained in continual use until it was replaced by the *James Stevens No.18*, pictured here, which served from 1902 until 1931. The *West Country and Galloway Journal* of Thursday, 21 January 1909 reported that there was a 'Famine on Ailsa Craig' – 'Late on Saturday night, at Girvan, a fire, the recognised signal for medical assistance, was observed on Ailsa Craig. At once the lifeboat crew were summoned as no other boat could venture the voyage and, the regular medical officer being unwell, Dr Nelson volunteered to go. On arriving at the Craig, after a rough passage, it was found that the quarrymen employed there had been out of provisions since Wednesday and that they had held a meeting among themselves, and, in defiance of the lighthouse keepers, had kindled the beacon, afterwards going to bed. On Sunday the storm continued, and the Ayr tug was chartered to take provisions across.'

The *Fairy Queen*, docked at the landing stage on the harbour side. In the background is the lifeboat house and the flagstaff. The harbour at Girvan was once proposed for development as the major ferry port to Ireland, but Stranraer, some forty miles further south, was eventually chosen. Stranraer was a sheltered port whereas Girvan was exposed to the strong westerly gales and as the harbour was located on the mouth of the Water of Girvan it required constant dredging to keep the channel clear. The decision in favour of Stranraer was ultimately reached when the railway was eventually extended there in 1877. The area in the background of this photograph has since been extensively developed and is now the site of amusement arcades, a car park, toilets, small gift shops, a swimming pool and pavilion, as well as a modern sewage pumping station. In the harbour a small jetty has also been constructed to allow small pleasure craft and yachts to moor safely.

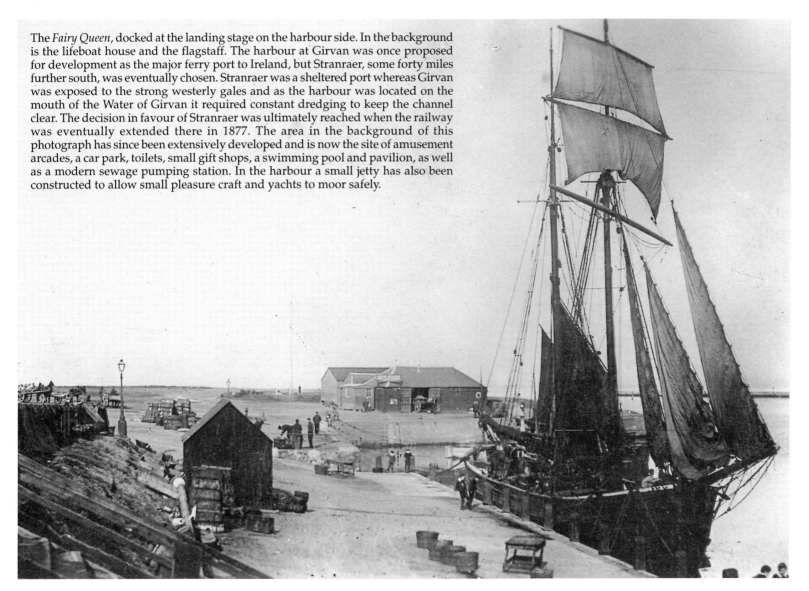

The Pier, Girvan.

The harbour at Girvan was originally constructed in 1824. In 1869 it was improved and in 1881 the pier and breakwater were built at a cost of £80,000. It was at this time that 'Scott's Hole' and the 'Red Man' were also constructed to protect the harbour from the strong north-westerly and south-westerly gales. 'Scott's Hole', the breakwater with the lighthouse, visible on the left of this photograph, took its name from its designer. The other breakwater, the 'Red Man', is out of picture to the right – it is uncertain how it acquired this name. A small fishing fleet was always based at the harbour in addition to the many small pleasure craft, but it was too small to accommodate many larger ships and subsequently trade was lost to the larger harbours at Ayr, Irvine and Troon. The main railway line from Glasgow originally only ran to the terminus just north of 'The Flushes', but it was later extended over the Water of Girvan to sidings that were built at Newton Kennedy, adjacent to the harbour side. This enabled coal to be unloaded into boats for shipment across the sea to Ireland, but the venture proved unsuccessful and any trade was eventually lost to the other harbours on the west coast.

CHURCH SQUARE, GIRVAN.

This photograph from around 1915 shows the view from Church Square looking westwards down into Hamilton Street towards 'Auld Stumpy'. On the right can be seen Macdonald's Central Bar, with the sign on the wall for the junction of High Street, which was one of the town's original streets. It was narrow in width with several even narrower closes and pends leading off from it and it was in this street that what was known as the 'Sanctuary Stone' stood. This oval-shaped, dark sea-green coloured block of whinstone, measuring 2 feet 4 inches by 2 feet 9 inches, owed its name to the fact that it was once a place of refuge to which debtors might flee and be safe when being pursued by their creditors. Those being pursued only had to place a foot on the stone to avoid being arrested. On the left of the photograph is the large ornamental Provost's Lantern which seems to be missing its centre lantern, no doubt due to some untoward accident! Today, High Street is now no more than a pedestrianised lane and the Central Bar has since been demolished.

Pictured on 14 July 1907, the musical church parade of the 76th Glasgow Company of the Boys' Brigade marches up through Hamilton Street and into Church Square towards St Andrew's United Presbyterian Church which was established in 1870 (it is located just out of picture on the left). The end of Hamilton Street leading up the slope to Church Square was once known as 'Kirk Brae' and it was at the top of this that the Parish Church once stood. This was built in 1780 to replace the original church, the remains of which can still be seen in the old kirkyard located just further north. In front of this church there also stood the old merket cross which was simply a rude block of stone. It was removed when the church was demolished in 1883 and the latter was replaced by a newer building erected close by in Montgomery Street. In 1911 the McCubbin fountain, gifted to the town by a local benefactor, Hugh McCubbin, was also sited in Church Square and replaced the Provost's Lantern which can be seen in the centre of this picture. Visible across the rooftops on the left is the McKechnie Institute and the Free Church in Dalrymple Street which was built in 1857, while 'Auld Stumpy' can be seen on the right.

Photographed outside his dressmaking and millinery shop at No. 2 Hamilton Street on 8 February 1904 is Mr Gilbert Pitt, with his wife and two sons. Gilbert Pitt, known by locals as 'Gib', also specialised in drapery and clothing and an advertisement in a local journal detailed what was on offer – 'Summer specialities in high-class fancy drapery – Ladies' blouses, gloves, veilings, lace goods – Gentlemen's caps, ties, collars – choice selection in the smartest of styles at city prices. Also golfing outfits.' He was also a well-known and well-liked personality within Girvan and was a 'first class elocutionist, raconteur and lightning artist' with a deep love of nature and children which he often reflected in poetry – a collection of his poems was published before his death in 1947. Other millinery shops in Girvan around this time included Thomas Young, General Draper, at 34 Dalrymple Street, where 'Hats, caps, collars, scarfs, braces, bathing outfits and every requisite for the summer season' was sold. There was also 'Special Value in Ladies' skirts and blouses. Millinery and dressmaking a speciality. A visit will be esteemed.' Miss Blane also had her Ladies' and Children's Outfitters shop at 24 Dalrymple Street, while next door at No. 25 was B.S. McLeary, another ladies' and children's outfitters.

13

Hamilton Street, looking west towards the junction with Knockushion Street around 1920. The street took its name from the family who bought the Bargany lands from the Kennedys in the eighteenth century and near the east end of the street the Bank Burn – or Mill Burn as it is locally known – flows directly underneath the road on its journey to join the Water of Girvan. It took the latter name from being the driving power for Girvan Mill which was located close to the town at the north corner of Victory Park, near the footbridge on the south side of the burn near Ballochtoul Castle. On the right of this photograph is the printing office of Smith and Gourlay, established in 1904, where, after 1910, the *Carrick Herald* was published each Friday. Other shops in the street at this time included Burgoyne's Bakery at No. 13, which was advertised as being 'The famous house for wedding cakes, Bermaline and Hovis bread daily. Dainty cakes for afternoon teas. Try our famed 'Ailsa' oatcakes. Superior to all others. Nice selection of high-class biscuits always in stock. Van delivers daily.' Also established in the street in 1882 was Wm. Paterson, painter, decorator, artist and colourman, whose premises were at No. 33. At No. 19 William Laing also established his electrical shop.

The heaviest snowfall ever recorded in Girvan occurred just after Christmas 1908 when, in common with all of Scotland, the town experienced a severe snowstorm and biting cold weather. On the left of this view showing 'The Cross', the snow can be seen piled high against the shop front of Robert and Tom McKechnie at No. 1 Dalrymple Street. They were tea and coffee merchants as well as importers of fine wines and brandies; they also blended selected Highland whiskies and had a large blending and bottling warehouse near the harbour. Souvenirs of Girvan and the surrounding district, including the renowned and popular 'Ailsa Craig Granite Jewellery', could be obtained from Farish the Jeweller's, who also had his shop at the Cross. The steeple – Auld Stumpy – dominates the photograph where a cart is turning from Knockushion Street into Dalrymple Street. It was built in 1827 to replace the old jail that stood on the site. The clock tower, gifted by Sir Hew Hamilton of Bargany, was added a few years later. The first, second and third floors contained prison cells, while the castellated parapet concealed the steeple bell. In the 1950s a weather vane was also installed. This area was known locally as 'The Cross' because it was where Bridge Street, Hamilton Street, Knockushion Street and Dalrymple Street all merged. Today this scene has changed greatly with 'Auld Stumpy' now standing in isolation after the McMaster Hall was pulled down following a disastrous fire in 1939.

The splendid McMaster Hall was gifted to the people of Girvan by Kirkoswald-born John McMaster who made his fortune as a Canterbury banker. The old rundown buildings that had surrounded 'Auld Stumpy' were demolished and in October 1909 Provost Alexander Telfer laid the foundation stone of the hall. On 17 August 1911 the opening ceremony was conducted by Provost McCreath with Mr McMaster in attendance. Built in the Renaissance style, with W.J. Jennings of Canterbury the architect and John Train and Taylor of Rutherglen the

builder, there was a lesser hall downstairs containing a piano and an organ, while an ornate wooden stairway led upstairs to the grand main hall and gallery that had seating for around 700 people. There was also a council chamber, police courtroom, dressing rooms and large and well-fitted cloakrooms for ladies and gentlemen. Two magnificent collections of pictures – one presented by Mr Thomas Davidson of Glasgow, originally a native of Girvan; and the other by Mr R. Edmiston of Glasgow – adorned the walls. Sadly the hall was devastated by a terrible fire in 1939 and remained in a derelict and dilapidated condition until 1956 when it was finally demolished to leave 'Auld Stumpy' standing isolated on the site. Stumpy Corner itself was once known locally as 'The Lazy Corner' due to the many local men who would frequent the spot and indulge in idle chat and gossip.

Dalrymple Street, pictured here after the tremendous snowfall of December 1908, with the view looking northwards towards Bridge Street and 'The Flushes'. On the right can be seen the sign advertising Lawson's Garage above the small lane which allowed access to the workshop located at the rear of the building. Adjacent is the ornamental façade and distinctive Corinthian doorway of the Bank of Scotland building which was opened in 1879. The following month the *Ayr Advertiser* of Thursday, 21 January 1909 reported that 'A daring burglary was last Wednesday committed at Primrose Bank, one of the villas on the golf course, the tenant of which is Mrs Kirkwood. Mrs Kirkwood resides in Largs and occupies the villa during the summer months. The place was left in charge of Mr McCallum, joiner, Wilson Street. The premises were all right on Wednesday last week, but on Thursday it was found that the house had been broken into, entrance having been gained by the window. The matter was reported to the police, and it was found that a gold watch and chain, a pair of gold sleeve links, and a lady's gold finger ring had been stolen. Information was circulated through the county by the constabulary and on Friday two men, named James and Joseph Boyce, were arrested in a public house in Kilmarnock while attempting to dispose of the watch and chain. The other articles have not yet been recovered.' The men were each later sentenced to four months imprisonment.

A view of Dalrymple Street from around 1900 and looking northwards towards the King's Arms Hotel and the Stumpy Corner. On the left can be seen the post office – Hugh McKenna was postmaster at this time – while adjacent is the small shop owned by M. Blane. On the right are the branches of the trees which surrounded the Free Church; Chalmers' Arcade now takes the site of both the trees and the church. Originally the building occupied by the post office housed a small grocer's store known as McKenna's and it was the son of the grocer who became the town's first postmaster. In 1837 Thomas Donaldson was the postmaster and at that time outgoing mail was despatched at quarter to eight every night, while letters arrived from Glasgow and England every night at quarter to twelve. Letters from Portpatrick also arrived nightly at quarter to eight and were despatched at quarter to twelve, while a penny-post to Barr operated every Monday, Wednesday and Friday mornings at eight. The appropriately named stagecoach, the 'Royal Mail', operated on this route and carried the mail.

Two large horse-drawn stagecoaches of the Girvan and Ballantrae Coaching Tour, pictured outside the King's Arms Hotel around 1900. The hotel was one of the largest in Girvan and was prominently situated at the top of Dalrymple Street. In a local journal published in 1922 it advertised its fifty bedrooms, lounge and smoking rooms and also mentioned the croquet and putting greens in its grounds. Some of the tariffs to guests at this time included – 'Inclusive Terms Per Day 15/-, Single bedroom (per night) 6/- to 7/-, Double bedroom (per night) 12/- to 20/-, Baths (Hot) 1/- and (Cold) 6d, Fires all day 3/- and at night 1/6 with visitors servants (per day) charging 10/6.' On the left, adjacent to the hotel, are the railings surrounding the entrance to the premises of the National Bank of Scotland. As a direct result of all the prosperity that was generated from the fishing and the handloom weaving there were as many as eight different banks established within the town at one time. These included the Hunters' and Company Bank, the Union Bank of Scotland Ltd, the Royal Bank of Scotland, the Commercial Bank of Scotland, the Ayrshire Banking Company, the Savings Bank of Glasgow and the British Linen Company Bank.

DALRYMPLE STREET, GIRVAN

For visitors to Girvan every sport and pastime was well catered for at C.M. Lawson's depot, opposite the post office in Dalrymple Street. In this photograph the gable sign can be seen on the right for Lawson's Garage where people could also hire motorcars, bicycles, mail carts and even invalid chairs. Previously, there had been a sign on the wall advertising the Carrick Cycle works. Opposite the King's Arms Hotel, at No. 13, were the premises of Blair and Son, drapers, clothiers, dressmakers, milliners and carpet warehousemen. Other shops in the street at this time included J. Glendinning – family grocer, provision merchant and Italian warehouseman at No. 29, and stationery and fancy goods were sold by Hugh Wallace, printer, stationer and bookseller, at No. 23 Dalrymple Street.

A group of local gentlemen, photographed in front of the general post office in the early 1900s. Visible in the background is D. McMaster's ironmongers shop. In the 1920s this business was owned by William Tait and was advertised in a local journal as being 'Girvan's Leading Hardware Shop – ironmongery, china and glass merchant – replace all your breakages at our stores – Visitors are well advised to visit our showrooms for ironmongery etc. Glass, china and earthenware. Crest china and souvenirs, E.P.N.S. and fancy goods.' Some of the other shops in the street at this time included Wm. A. Doig's Jewellery Depot at No. 4 where holidaymakers could purchase local souvenirs and Ailsa Craig jewellery, while at No. 59 were the Central Provision Stores – 'the most central grocery and provision warehouse in town' – with James McCrindle as proprietor. Gib Graham, the chemist, had his Pharmacy at No. 32, which was the third shop south from the post office. A.G.B. Paterson, dispensing and photographic chemist, was located at 'The Medical Hall' at No. 39. His wares included 'drugs, sundries, toilet requisites, specialities, water softener, cucumber jelly, skin cream and toilet oatmeal'.

On the left is the McKechnie Institute which was designed by James McKissack in the Scottish baronial style with a balustraded octagonal tower. It comprised a library and reading room and was opened in Dalrymple Street in December 1888. It was gifted to the town from a bequest of £6,500 left by local wine and spirit merchants Mr Thomas and Robert McKechnie, who ran a high-class grocery business at the corner of Dalrymple Street. They also left £2,000 to provide bursaries for two Girvan youths in Glasgow University and also £1,000 to the poor and needy of the parish. The library originally contained upwards of 5,000 well-chosen volumes and readers paid an annual fee of five shillings. The institute also contained two reading rooms, a billiard room containing two tables, and an attached house for the librarian. The building was erected at a cost of £3,000 and is still in use as a local museum and exhibition centre. Also on the left is James Crosbie's fine china and ironmonger's shop (established in 1826), while across the street is the distinctive frontage of the Tower Warehouse. James Crosbie later purchased the premises of the Maybole Shoe Shop at No. 42; advertising as 'the store with the clock', he stocked ironmongery on the ground floor and china and glassware on the first floor.

Looking south along Dalrymple Street with the junction for Ailsa Street East (which was formerly known as Plum Street) on the left, while opposite is Ailsa Street West leading down to 'The Green'. In 1951 there were a staggering 126 shops in Girvan, including six bakers, five butchers, eleven cafés, four chemists, seven coal merchants, five confectioners, seven drapers and five fish and chip shops. These shops included the 'popular' Drapery Warehouse at No. 35, where dressmaking and millinery was undertaken with ladies' lace collars, blouses and corsets a speciality. It was renowned as the best shop in town for ready-mades and sold goods at the lowest prices for cash only – John McPhail was the fancy draper and the proprietor. Robert Hervey also owned the similarly named Tower Drapery Warehouse at No. 43 and at No. 26 Thom Bros.' family grocers and merchants sold wine, tea and spirits.

Photographed in June 1918, the large motorised funeral procession of Captain Ian H.D. Henderson of the Argyll and Sutherland Highlanders Regiment travels slowly southwards along Dalrymple Street as it heads to- wards the Doune Cemetery. Seconded to the Royal Air Force, Captain Henderson had been killed at Turnberry, although the cause of his death was not publicised. The previous year two auxiliary schools of

aerial gunnery had been established at Turnberry to teach young pilots gunnery, bombing and air combat skills. The casualty rate at the schools was high and the school eventually closed in 1945. A monument was later erected at Turnberry next to the old aerodrome which is inscribed 'To the memory of the officers, non-commissioned officers, and men of the Royal Flying Corps, Royal Air Force, and Australian and United States Air Services who gave their lives for their country while serving in the School of Aerial Gunnery and Fighting'. The names of thirty-nine men are inscribed on this monument.

The young men of the Royal Scots Fusiliers march through the streets of Girvan on their way to war in 1914. The town has seen many turbulent times in the past, particularly during the nineteenth century. One notable event is commemorated by a small stone that stands on the west side of the main road, just one hundred yards north of the railway bridge. Alexander Ross's stone stands at what is known locally as the 'Sheddings of the Road' and was erected at the exact spot where this constable was shot dead in 1831 while attempting to prevent a procession of Ulster Orangemen from entering the town. Two Orange lodges were established within Girvan due to the influx, from the 1780s onwards, of many Ulster immigrants attempting to find work as handloom weavers. On 25 April 1831 conflict engulfed the town when the Orangemen attacked a procession of Reform Bill supporters, causing the magistrates to ban all subsequent processions. However, tremendous rioting took place on 12 July, during which Special Constable Ross was shot dead by Samuel Waugh, a former member of the County Down Militia. Waugh was subsequently hanged in Ayr for the murder and at the junction of the roads to New Dailly and Maybole the small memorial stone was erected. In the 1980s a new roundabout was built at this busy junction and the stone was subsequently moved twice to its present position.

Members of the Cadet Battalion R.S.F. Girvan High School Corps are pictured outside the former High School that was built of red sandstone by William Cowie in 1912. The people of Girvan, old and young alike, adopted numerous interests such as the boy scouts and the brownies. Other organisations included the Carrick Fishing Club, the Masons (Girvan St. John's Lodge), the Amateur Dramatic Society, the Choral Society, the International Friendship League, Girvan High School Football Club, the Debating Society and the Chess Club. The High School Corps encouraged numerous young boys to enlist into the Territorials and many served honourably for the Royal Scots Fusiliers during both the First and Second World Wars.

An unfortunate young man receives a good soaking during one of the many special events and games held during the 'Victory Sports' of 1919. These were held in Victory Park on what was appropriately called 'Victory Day'. Complete with its bandstand, the twenty-two acre park was gifted to the town by Colonel North Victor Cecil Dalrymple Hamilton of Bargany to commemorate the conclusion of the First World War. It is the most recently acquired of Girvan's parks and is situated in the Holm of Ballochtoul behind Dalrymple Street, with entrance from Ailsa Street East and Wesley Road. In the seventeenth century this was where the Tower of Ballochtoul stood. It was a monument of the builder's folly, being raised five storeys high without a staircase and with only one room in each storey, and while it stood in the midst of rich cornfields, it had neither a garden nor orchard. The builder of this remarkable, if impractical, house was Boyd of Penkill.

This photograph shows the 'Victory Fête' that was held on 23 July 1919 at the Bowling Green. In 1668 when Girvan was granted a charter to form a burgh of barony, an additional charter for the rights and privileges to hold regular fairs was also granted. The Girvan Fair was held twice annually on the first Monday of April and on the first Monday of October and soon grew to surpass even the legendary 'Kirkdandie', the annual fair at the village of Barr. Great crowds from all parts flocked to attend and, even as late as 1890, it was difficult to walk along Main Street which was packed with countryside visitors looking at all manner of colourful stalls selling everything from sweets to merchandise, and the street entertainments provided by musicians and minstrels. Around 1840 John McCartney wrote a ballad entitled 'Girvan Fair' in recognition of its importance and in it he described how people travelled from all areas to attend: 'Oh there were folk frae Ballantrae/And some frae far Stranraer, sir/Frae Minnibole and Colmonell/Kirkoswald and the Barr, sir/Frae Weary Neuk and Dinnimuck/An a' alang the shore, sir/And sic a crowd in Girvan toon/Was never seen before, sir.'

The Countess of Stair gifted Stair Park to the town in 1875 and at the southern end of the park a magnificent ornamental bandstand and tea kiosk were constructed. In this photograph a large crowd of young children have gathered around the bandstand and tearooms to watch the popular Hampson's Pierrots perform. Many musical companies conducted variety entertainments here while the audience could enjoy tea and light refreshments. Visible in the background are the attractive houses on Henrietta Street and the small gasometer of the gas works. On the right, behind the bandstand, is the wall of the Doune Cemetery. In 1922 a large granite obelisk war memorial designed by James A. Morris was erected in the middle of the park to commemorate the 157 men who lost their lives in the First World War; a further fifty-six names were added after the Second World War. This photograph appeared on a postcard, dated 8 March 1910, which was sent from the Police Office at Girvan to Miss Duncan at Glen Clova in Forfarshire. The postcard was one of the popular 'Caledonia' or 'Ailsa Series' that were printed and sold by W. Gilmour in Girvan.

By around the 1890s Girvan began to transform from a traditional weaving and fishing village into a popular coastal holiday resort. During the Boer War at the turn of the twentieth century the first open-air entertainers arrived to perform to the increasing number of summer holidaymakers. Hampson's Pierrots were a troupe of 'black-faced' minstrels led by Hamish McLean and his deputy Sam Haslam, and initially their platform was a small portable wooden square that was laid out in one of the sandy hollows in Stair Park. At first the shows only came for just a week or so, but later they started to stay from the middle of June until the end of August. The Dennistoun Amateur Minstrels were another group of pierrots who travelled to Girvan to work through the season. They performed twice a day regardless of the weather and their takings were simply money donated by the audience during and after their shows. In 1909 members included Johnnie Blair, Robert Stewart, Alexander Watson, Archie McLay, Thomas S. Bourne, Jay Brown, J. H. Pickney and Sydney Barr. Other names associated with travelling entertainments and shows went on to become household names in the town, including Paris, Cook, Biddal, Graham, Cooper and Boswell.

THE · CANADIAN · CAVALIERS
BAND · STAND · GIRVAN

Musicians of the Canadian Cavaliers, photographed on the stage of the bandstand in Stair Park. Initially all of the shows and musical entertainments held in Girvan were staged at 'The Flushes', the triangle of vacant ground at the northern end of the town which is now the site of Bridge Street, with attractions such as Wilmot's Galloping Horses on a large carousel roundabout proving highly popular. A large steam engine powered the machine which could carry over one hundred passengers. Other attractions included the Swallow Cocks and Hens, the Bicycle Ride and later the Cake Walk, Chair-o-planes, Jumping Horses, Hey Day, Mont Blanc, Waltzer, Big Wheel, Dodgem Cars and the Helter Skelter. Just after the turn of the century the amusements, stalls and rides moved from 'The Flushes' to the harbour area where large marquees and stalls could be erected for several months during the summer. Many of the travelling showmen enjoyed the benefit of being able to stay in the one place for longer but unfortunately, with the subsequent development of the harbour area and the Beach Pavilion, many of the shows were never to be seen in Girvan again. However, some entertainers such as the Lawrences and the Brownes did have the foresight to take their amusements under cover.

Adjacent to Stair Park are Nos. 153 and 124–142 Henrietta Street, which was named after the late Duchess de Coigny, one of the Bargany family members who were at one time the superiors of the town. It was here that the council built some 600 houses during the inter-war years. Designed by the architect Thomas Taylor of Hutton these were Girvan's first council houses to be built according to the English style of street planning. This photograph shows Provost Smellie opening the burgh houses in October 1921. At this time many new streets were being built as the town's reputation as a holiday resort grew steadily and the population increased to around 7,300. Henrietta Street was at one time graced with sycamore trees enclosed in ornamental railings, but these have almost all disappeared today. With a one-way system for traffic now operating within the town Henrietta Street carries all traffic travelling northwards from Stranraer and Newton Stewart.

Davidson Cottage Hospital, Girvan

The Davidson Cottage Hospital was gifted to the town by Miss Jessie Davidson and Messrs Thomas and James Davidson to honour the memory of their mother, Mrs Margaret Davidson. Designed by Watson Salmond & Gray and built on The Avenue from grey Auchenheath stone, it was officially opened by Thomas Davidson on 16 June 1922. It contained two wards of four beds each, two private wards, an operating theatre and also staff rooms. At the time a fund was also established for its continued upkeep. The hospital is still in use and the Davidson Trust fund still operates within the town. In the corner of the photograph is the seal of Girvan, which depicts a three-masted ship in full sail with pennons flying, and the town's motto, *Sigillun Burgi De Girvan* – 'ever sailing, never sinking'. Unfortunately, this seal is by no means officially heraldic and was merely adopted by the burgh as an appropriate symbol. However, many of the old street names of the town were derived from the fishing industry – Windy Row, Sandy Row, Tarry Lane, Wapping Lane, The Trough, The Wrack Road, Blue Sky and Skipper Row are all expressive of lives dependent on the sea.

Mourners gather to hear the prayer at the funeral, held at the Doune Cemetery, of Mr William Jackson, composer of the music for 'The Bonnie Lass O' Ballochmyle'. There are two graveyards within the town; the newer one, pictured here, was opened adjacent to the old gas works between Stair Park and the Doune Park. The older graveyard is located just off Old Street and once contained the original parish church. This is entered through a large red sandstone archway, designed by James A. Morris, which was erected in memory of William Johnston in 1908. Johnston, a renowned and well-liked member of the community, had died in 1838 and the archway was bequeathed by his son, Alexander. This was the old Kirk Port of its day and it is still possible today to see the site of the original church which apparently was 50 feet long by 28 feet wide and seated 500 persons. It has been estimated that in the little half acre of ground some 20,000 persons lie buried, most notably several parish ministers. Mr Thomas McKechnie who founded the McKechnie Institute and Alexander Ross, the special constable shot in 1831, also lie there. On the left of this photograph, standing amongst the mourners, is Mr Gilbert Pitt, a well-known and much liked character within Girvan, who owned a dressmaking and millinery shop in Hamilton Street.

Girvan's excellent boating lake was designed in 1938 by James Wright in collaboration with the council. It was built on 'The Green', just south from the harbour, and was distinctive with its small island in the centre, incorporating the glider dome, and its own fleet of motorboats for hire. Adjacent was the smaller children's yachting pond, while on the far right can be seen the parking area next to the harbour side. Also visible is the distinctive granite ornamental fountain, crowned with a large anchor and chain, erected in April 1927 by Mrs Crauford McCracken of Moorston to honour the memory of her parents, Alexander Clachar, sea captain and ship owner, and his wife. Little has changed in this scene today, although the little island has since been extensively landscaped with shrubs, the children's pond has become a small play-park, and the boats are now powered by peddles rather than motors.

Girvan Sands run for about a mile and a half from the harbour all the way southwards to Shalloch and were a major part of Girvan's appeal to holidaymakers. At Shalloch there was a 'smiddy' or smithy which was formerly a saltpan house employed in the manufacture of salt from the seawater. A corn mill was also located here, on the Girvan to Ballantrae road, and was driven by the water from the Byne Burn which flows down the glen skirting the base of the Byne Hill. In the background a farmer can be seen with horse and cart, possibly gathering seaweed which was used to fertilise land for agriculture. Wrack Road, now known as Wreck Road, was the route taken during the eighteenth century by farmers conveying seaweed from the shore to manure the surrounding fields.

On warm summer days many visitors flocked to enjoy the sandy beach and the bathing station just off the promenade. The seventeen individual bathing boxes and screens were located just below the promenade on the beach front, while at either end were the toilets and changing rooms for the men and women. The boxes were supervised by attendants and the charges and terms for their use were very moderate. It was estimated that from April through to October as many as 4,000 people would visit the town and at the height of the season, during the Glasgow Fair fortnight, the influx of visitors was nearer 10,000. Although the bathing boxes are now closed and the toilets demolished, the promenade is still lit at night and has ample seating for visitors.

During the height of the summer season the putting green and sea front at Girvan always proved very popular with holidaymakers and in this photograph from 1933 people can be seen thronging the promenade, which runs south from the harbour all the way to Shalloch. On the right can be seen the large open expanse of common grass, known as 'The Green', which was once used by fisherman for stringing out their nets, by womenfolk for drying their washing and by the weavers for bleaching and drying their cloths. In 1938 it was landscaped to incorporate the boating lake. Clearly visible in the water is the wooden lifeguard and diving platform. The *Ayr Advertiser* of Thursday, 19 July 1905 reported on a remarkable 'Bathing Mishap' – 'While a young lady visitor to Girvan was bathing between the bathing station and the quay, she got into difficulties through becoming entangled in the seaweed which near the quay is very plentiful. Her cries soon attracted attention and she was quickly brought ashore, but was unconscious. Harbourmaster McCreadie and Mr Muir, coxswain of the Girvan lifeboat, set to work to bring back the girl to consciousness and it was only after a half hour's work that this was accomplished. She was afterwards able to proceed home.'

With its towering rocky cliffs, Ailsa Craig rises to a height of 1,114 feet, is 3,900 feet in length and 2,600 feet in breadth, and has a circumference of approximately 2 ½ miles. It covers a total area of 220 acres. Photographed in 1914 are the ruins of the strongly-built castle on its south-east side. Clinging precariously to a rocky ledge 400 feet high, the three-storey tower, which is 30 feet in height, is possibly of sixteenth century origin. During the summer many holidaymakers undertook the excursion from Girvan to Ailsa Craig. Two paths led directly to the summit – 'The Highlandman's Road', a dangerous zig-zagging path only for those with a cool head and a steady foot, and the more gentle, slanting route that leads to the castle which is located on a flat area called the 'Castle Comb'. Original ownership of the castle is indicated by markings on a wall showing three cinque-foils arranged in the form of a letter 'V', the symbol of the once powerful Hamilton family. The Craig is formed from very hard fine-grained granite and from the 1880s this was quarried to manufacture curling stones. The stone was taken to Mauchline where it was shaped, polished and finished. In the 1950s some 3,000 stones were being produced annually, and while mass production ceased commercially in 1971, quarrying on the Craig has again started on a very small scale and the stones are still fashioned in Mauchline.

While residing at Ardmillan Castle, Mr William Morton of Moseley, Birmingham, gave a generous donation of 1,000 guineas to the Girvan Bowling Club to develop sporting facilities within the town. The Morton Recreational Grounds were subsequently formed just off The Avenue and these included four tennis courts, two six-rink bowling greens and a croquet lawn. The grounds were very popular and were later advertised in the *Carrick Herald* as being delightfully situated in attractive grounds with two bowling greens, five tennis courts and a putting green. From May to September the grounds were open daily from 10.30 a.m. to 9 p.m. and offered the visitor open tournaments and competitions throughout the season, in addition to teas and light refreshments. Today the tennis courts and bowling greens are still popular with locals and visitors.

Girvan Bowling Club was formed on 21 July 1841 when, after a general meeting in the King's Arms Hotel, the rules were established and the laws of the game read and approved. The first green was located behind the present Royal Bank of Scotland building and subscriptions were set at five shillings, payable in two instalments (a large sum in those days), with membership limited to fifty in number. The first competitive game took place on 14 August between the Married Men and the Bachelors, with the latter winning by ten shots. In 1842 Robert McKechnie won the championship and was presented with a set of prize bowls. In 1897 the club moved to The Avenue and two years later amalgamated with the Victoria Club, although it kept its original name. A new clubhouse was built in 1936, incorporating changing rooms, lounge and veranda, and in 1941 the centenary was celebrated. Only eight years later the club was expanded to have four greens – No. 1, named Bargany; No. 2, named Glendoune; No. 3, named Trochrague; and No. 4, named Dalquharran. In this photograph a competition is underway at the club on 24 May 1910. The photograph appeared on a postcard which was addressed to a Miss Dickie at 18 Clark Terrace, Kilmarnock, and carried the message: 'Do you recognise Marjorie in this? She is always at the front you know. The sun was here, but unfortunately the weather seems to have broken.'

'This is one of Glasgow's summer resorts, it has a beautiful beach for bathing, also fine roads for cycling' is the message written on the back of this old postcard dating from around 1911 and sent to an address in Wellington, New Zealand. This view shows the railway station that was built at the eastern end of Vicarton Street. The waiting rooms and platforms are clearly visible adjacent to the track, as is the small underpass which allowed passengers to safely reach the other side of the line. Horse-drawn carriages wait patiently to convey the disembarking passengers into the town centre. The line was originally opened in 1869, with the terminus being located just north of 'The Flushes' (the open area which once existed near Bridge Street), but when the Girvan and Portpatrick Junction Railway was completed to Stranraer in 1877 this station was built. For many years the line was hampered by operational and financial difficulties and by 1892 it had been taken over by the Glasgow and South Western Railway. In 1946 the railway station was completely rebuilt and modernised.

Dickie's Garage in Old Street was Girvan's first ever garage and was the sole agent for Rover motors. In the lower photograph, dating from 1920, Mr Robin Dickie can be seen standing inside the garage with his mechanics and staff. They maintained and serviced the many vehicles that crowded the Girvan streets throughout the season as well as offering services to motorists travelling to and from Stranraer.

The Hamilton Arms Hotel is located at Nos. 12–22 Bridge Street, near the Flushes Bridge. A long-established, family-run business, it has its own car park, two bars, several rooms to let and a large function/dining room. Despite the fact that the main industry of the town was catering for the tremendous influx of visitors during the summer months, there were no large hotels or boarding establishments in the town. The largest of the five hotels had only thirty-five bedrooms to let and the fifty or so boarding houses were almost all small private residential houses that had been converted to accommodate visitors. Most of the holidaymakers found lodgings in private apartments, a practice dating back to at least 1827 when Robert Chambers, while visiting the town, wrote: 'Instead of finding any inconvenience from the crowded state of his house, the Milesian of Girvan who is so unfortunate as to have a whole room for his family feels disagreeably lonesome, and either advertises half a house to let, or hangs out a ticket informing the passing traveller that he can give him lodging for the night.' This photograph shows the garage and pavement petrol pump that were once at the Hamilton Arms. For many years a strange metal ring could also be seen hanging on the outside of the hotel wall – at one time this was used for tying up horses in the street.

AYRSHIRE POTATO SEASON GIRVAN 1901

This photograph shows many of the wealthy and well-dressed local farmers, agents and buyers that were involved in the growing of early potatoes in the fields surrounding the Girvan district.

The harvesting of early-season potatoes was carried out extensively in the coastal fields surrounding Girvan and in 1837 'an immense quantity' (some 300 tons) of potatoes was shipped overseas to places such as America and other parts of the British Isles from the harbour at Girvan. The introduction of more productive varieties saw yields steadily increase and by 1905 some 13,000 tons of potatoes passed through the Goods and Harbour Branch of the Girvan Railway. If the weather was favourable the crop was ready to be lifted before the end of June and the growers were often forced to hire as many as forty to fifty carts from neighbouring farms to transport the crop to the railway or to local markets. The potatoes would be sold at auction to merchants or privately on a per acre basis as grown, with prices varying from £30–£40 in 1914 to £150 during the First World War and increasing to £200 by the early 1950s. In this photograph from 1913 many of the local farmers are pictured at Girvan's goods station. The railway line is in the background and the houses across the river on Watermouth Park are also visible.

The fertile, sandy and well-drained soil near the coast, combined with the mild spring climate, the frequent rainfall and the comparative absence of frost during April and May, proved to be excellent conditions for the growing of potatoes. When all of these conditions proved ideal, a saleable crop could be harvested much earlier in the season than anywhere else in Scotland, with the result that early Ayrshire potatoes were much in demand. Many varieties were grown with fanciful names such as 'Rocks', 'Redbogs', Dalmahoy', 'Goodrich', 'Fiftyfold', 'Dons', 'Jubilee' and 'Puritan', but near the end of the nineteenth century the 'Epicure' potato was introduced and from that time onwards yields increased dramatically all along the coast. Grown continually year after year in the same fields, the yields began to reduce after 1923. This allowed other competitors to enter the marketplace, but today potatoes are still grown widely in the fields all along the coast. In this scene the potato harvesters are hard at work in the fields near Girvan. The wooden barrel on the right would have been used to transport the potatoes before bags or sacks were introduced in 1939.

Located just to the south of Girvan is the distinctive outline of Byne Hill, beneath which the town's first camping site was established. Photographed around 1920, camping at the site proved to be very popular with the many holidaymakers who flocked to the town during the summer months. At the top of the hill is a cairn which was erected by the local Round Table to commemorate the Queen's Jubilee in 1977, while further south, on the saddle-shaped part of the hill, there is another monument in the form of an obelisk that was erected to honour the memory of Major Archibald Craufuird from nearby Ardmillan House. He served extensively with the army in India and was involved in the landing at and capture of the Cape of Good Hope in 1795. Today the site of the campsite contains Byne Hill Cemetery. In 1828 copper was mined – unprofitably – on the south side of the hill.